TEENS IN FINLAND

Teens in FINLAND

by Jason Skog

Content Adviser: Sirpa Tuomainen,
Lecturer of Finnish Studies,
University of California, Berkeley

Reading Adviser: Alexa Sandmann, Ed.D.,
Professor of Literacy,
Kent State University

Compass Point Books ✦ Minneapolis, Minnesota

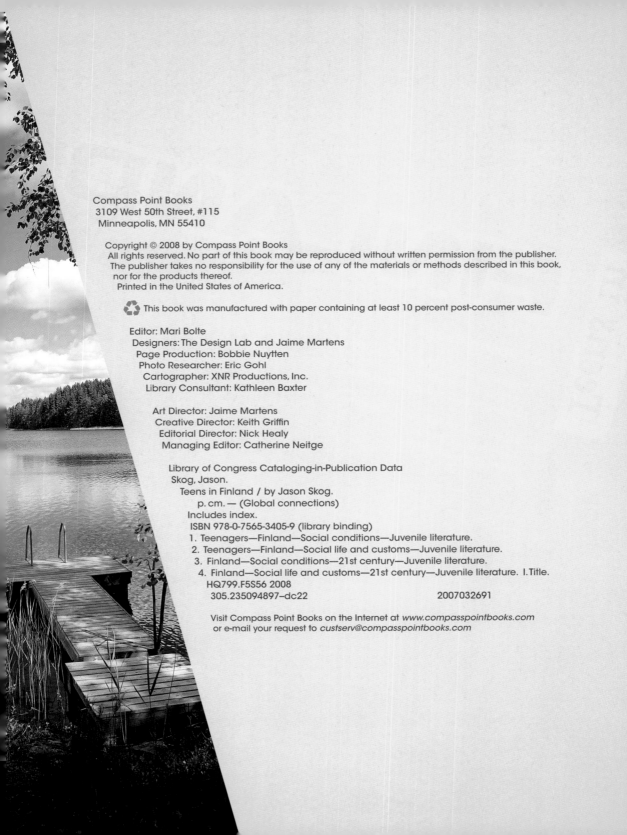

Compass Point Books
3109 West 50th Street, #115
Minneapolis, MN 55410

Editor: Mari Bolte
Designers: The Design Lab and Jaime Martens
Page Production: Bobbie Nuytten
Photo Researcher: Eric Gohl
Cartographer: XNR Productions, Inc.
Library Consultant: Kathleen Baxter

Art Director: Jaime Martens
Creative Director: Keith Griffin
Editorial Director: Nick Healy
Managing Editor: Catherine Neitge

Library of Congress Cataloging-in-Publication Data
Skog, Jason.
    Teens in Finland / by Jason Skog.
        p. cm. — (Global connections)
    Includes index.
    ISBN 978-0-7565-3405-9 (library binding)
        1. Teenagers—Finland—Social conditions—Juvenile literature.
        2. Teenagers—Finland—Social life and customs—Juvenile literature.
        3. Finland—Social conditions—21st century—Juvenile literature.
        4. Finland—Social life and customs—21st century—Juvenile literature. I. Title.
    HQ799.F5S56 2008
        305.235094897—dc22   2007032691

Visit Compass Point Books on the Internet at *www.compasspointbooks.com*
or e-mail your request to *custserv@compasspointbooks.com*

Table of Contents

ICELAND

SCOTLAND

NORTHERN
IRELAND

IRELAND

ENGLAND

WALES

ATLANTIC
OCEAN

FRANCE

ANDORRA

PORTUGAL

SPAIN

Canary Islands

MOROCCO

ALGERIA

WESTERN SAHARA

MAURITANIA

MALI

SENEGAL

BRAZIL

GUINEA BISSAU

GUINEA

BURKINA
FASO

Helsinki

SIERRA LEONE

BENIN

TOGO

LIBERIA

IVORY COAST

NIGE

GHANA

EQUATORIAL

SAO TOME & PRINC

ATLANTIC
OCEAN

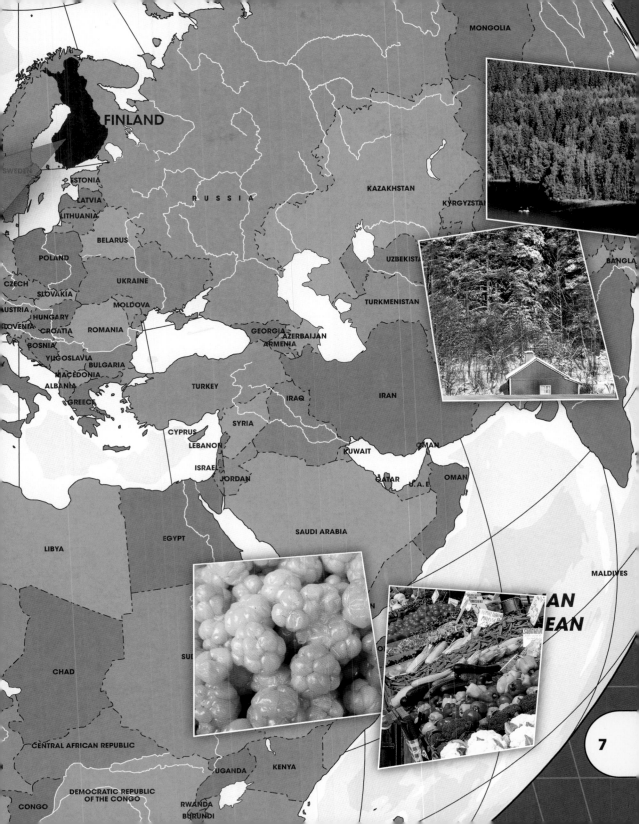

FINLAND

SWEDEN

ESTONIA
LATVIA
LITHUANIA

R U S S I A

KAZAKHSTAN

KYRGYZSTAN

MONGOLIA

BELARUS

POLAND

CZECH

SLOVAKIA

UKRAINE

AUSTRIA

HUNGARY

SLOVENIA

MOLDOVA

CROATIA

ROMANIA

BOSNIA

YUGOSLAVIA

MACEDONIA

BULGARIA

ALBANIA

GREECE

TURKEY

CYPRUS

LEBANON

ISRAEL

JORDAN

SYRIA

IRAQ

GEORGIA

AZERBAIJAN

ARMENIA

TURKMENISTAN

UZBEKISTAN

IRAN

KUWAIT

QATAR

U.A.E.

OMAN

OMAN

SAUDI ARABIA

BANGLA

MALDIVES

LIBYA

EGYPT

CHAD

SU

CENTRAL AFRICAN REPUBLIC

UGANDA

KENYA

AN
EAN

7

CONGO

DEMOCRATIC REPUBLIC
OF THE CONGO

RWANDA

BURUNDI

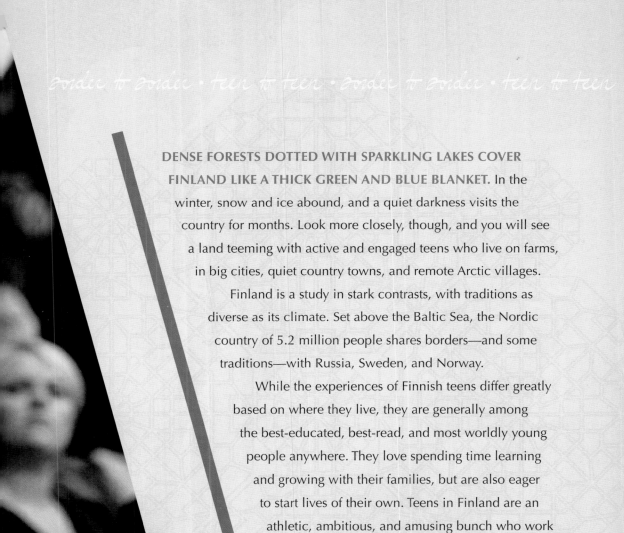

DENSE FORESTS DOTTED WITH SPARKLING LAKES COVER FINLAND LIKE A THICK GREEN AND BLUE BLANKET. In the winter, snow and ice abound, and a quiet darkness visits the country for months. Look more closely, though, and you will see a land teeming with active and engaged teens who live on farms, in big cities, quiet country towns, and remote Arctic villages.

Finland is a study in stark contrasts, with traditions as diverse as its climate. Set above the Baltic Sea, the Nordic country of 5.2 million people shares borders—and some traditions—with Russia, Sweden, and Norway.

While the experiences of Finnish teens differ greatly based on where they live, they are generally among the best-educated, best-read, and most worldly young people anywhere. They love spending time learning and growing with their families, but are also eager to start lives of their own. Teens in Finland are an athletic, ambitious, and amusing bunch who work hard and play even harder.

More than 586,000 students are enrolled annually in Finland's nearly 3,700 primary schools.

1

School Is Serious Work

THE HOUSE IS DARK AND QUIET IN THE EARLY WINTER MORNING. The alarm clock signals the start of the day well before sunrise. Parents rise and rouse a couple of cranky teens from their deep slumber: "Hyvää huomenta!", or "Good morning!" It's time to get dressed, eat a big breakfast, and say goodbye. The teens load piles of books and papers into their backpacks, bundle up in warm coats and hats, and head out the door for a short walk to school.

The Finns take education very seriously. All Finns can read—the country's investment in the education system is higher than that of any other developed country. Every year, Finland spends 7 percent of its gross domestic product on teaching its children.

Access to schools is relatively good despite the fact that Finland's population is scattered throughout the country. More than 80 percent of Finnish students live less than three miles (five kilometers)

Hyvää huomenta
(hyu-vah-huoh-men-ta)

11

from their school. In those cases, getting to and from school is the responsibility of the students and their families. Because so many students live close enough to walk, school buses are rare.

However, for some students in northern Finland, the traveling distance to school is farther—sometimes as much as 45 miles (72 km). Transportation is provided for students who live farther than three miles (five km) from school.

School Starts at 6

Finnish children are able to start attending preschool when they turn 6 years old. During that first year, they are taught to work in teams, share, and follow instructions. The focus is on play, with little focus on learning. While there has been some discussion about making them attend school earlier, the Finns believe it's important to let children be children. As a result, Finnish children are allowed to play and learn on their

Libraries and Reading

The number of newspapers and books printed per person each year in Finland makes the nation one of the most well-read countries in the world. Finns also have one of the best library systems in the world, and they use it. Every year the average Finn visits the library 13 times and borrows 21 items.

Although preschool in Finland is voluntary, at least 90 percent of all children attend. The majority of preschool education is given in day care centers.

own during their early years. By the age of 7, most of them are able to read and count.

When they turn 7, Finnish children begin the first year of nine required years of schooling, also called comprehensive school. The nine-month school year runs from mid-August through May.

Lessons begin between 8 and 10 A.M. each day and end between 1 and 4 P.M. Classes last around 45 minutes, lunch is 30 minutes, and a 15-minute break for recess follows lunch. Younger students are required to go outside into the play yard for recess. For those with longer school days, a snack is usually served in the afternoon.

Comprehensive-school subjects include language, literature, environmental study, civics, religion or ethics, history, social studies, mathematics, physics, chemistry, biology, geography, physical education, music, handicrafts, art, and home economics.

Teen Scenes

In the predawn hours, a chilly wind whips across the Lapland prairie as a 15-year-old Sami boy rises for the start of the day. The Sami people have lived in northern Finland's Lapland region since ancient times, and many of their traditions remain. Outside, the temperature is freezing cold, but inside, the boy's father has already stoked a roaring fire. The boy devours a quick breakfast of porridge and sausage before walking to school for a full day of classes. In the afternoon, he squeezes in a quick game of floor ball, an indoor type of hockey, in the school gym with his friends. In the evening, he returns to work with his father on their reindeer farm, tending to the herd.

In Finland's rural midsection, a 14-year-old girl wants to sleep in, but her mother wakes her early to walk the dog. Then, after her own quick meal of cereal, fresh berries covered in milk or yogurt, and a glass of juice, she dresses for school. She takes a 20-minute taxi ride to school. After school, she meets up with her cross-country ski team to swoosh along the trails in the woods nearby. When she returns home, the girl tackles her homework before helping her mother set the table for dinner. After she eats, she relaxes with a favorite novel and drifts off to sleep.

In Helsinki, the hustle and bustle of the traffic outside his apartment wakes a 16-year-old boy before his alarm rings. His mother and father are already dressed for work, and he takes a quick shower before downing a slice of toasted rye bread with garlic-flavored cream cheese and turkey, a banana, and a tall glass of orange juice. He doesn't want to be late to meet his friends outside for their walk to school a few blocks away. When the school day ends, he heads off to the swimming pool for a few laps and then goes to hockey practice.

While they live in different parts of the country, teens around Finland share a dedication to learning and a passion for physical fitness. They work hard to keep their minds alert and their bodies active.

Students begin learning foreign languages as soon as they begin comprehensive school. Their first foreign language is usually Swedish, which is an official language of Finland, along with Finnish. However, students can begin with English or French. In addition, they begin learning two or three other foreign languages—German, Spanish, Japanese, or perhaps Russian. Which language, or languages, a student chooses depends heavily on what the school has to offer.

The government has worked to make sure students in rural areas have the same access to modern technology as those in the cities. Today most Finnish students have access to computers and the Internet at school, and many of them have the same opportunities at home.

Classrooms are equipped with an overhead projector and a chalkboard.

Most classrooms also have computers, a TV, a video projector, and a DVD or CD player. For science class, there is lab equipment. For Finnish class, there are collections of short stories and novels. Every school has a gymnasium for physical education.

Not every school has a library, however, because the network of local public libraries is so strong. Students can check out materials from the community library after school on their way home.

While the standards for education are the same throughout Finland, each school system creates its own set of courses and decides how they are taught. It's also up to the students themselves. They play an active role in deciding what subjects they take and how they are taught. Students help to make education policy at all levels of learning. This approach appears to be

Finns are among the heaviest users of mobile communication technology in the world.

15

There are nearly 1,000 libraries across the country. Every community has a library. They're getting fuller every year—more than 14,000 new titles are published in Finland every year.

paying off. Finnish students often score at the top in math, language, and science tests compared with other pupils around the world.

In the classroom, students call teachers by their first names, according to Finnish custom. Teachers more often lead discussions than give lectures. They invite the students to speak up and participate. There is an emphasis on "active learning"—doing something related to the subject—rather than reading or talking about it.

Yum! It's Lunchtime

Every student in Finland gets a free hot meal at lunchtime. Students take a break from their studies and head to the cafeteria, some of which have small, cozy tables covered with a tablecloth and set with a vase of flowers.

Students grab a lunch tray and line up at the counter to get their plates of food. A typical hot lunch is "meatballs and mash," which consists of meatballs on top of mashed potatoes. It's been a favorite of children for many genera-

A Brief History of Finland

Finnish people were first recorded by the Roman historian Tacitus in 98 A.D. The first modern Finns arrived as missionaries and crusaders from Sweden in 1155. The country was ruled by the Swedish until the 19th century. In 1809, Russia won the Finnish War and in turn became the controller of the country.

In 1906 Finland created its own national parliament, and on December 6, 1917, it became an independent country. The 1952 Summer Olympic Games were held in Helsinki, and the country officially became a part of the United Nations in 1955. The euro was adopted as the only form of currency in 2002, and Finland is one of 15 countries to use the euro.

tions. They might also have a salad, bread, and milk with their meal.

At some Finnish schools, students are required to help with chores. They are expected to learn by doing various jobs with various people, not always their teacher. They might work with the librarian, helping put books back on the shelves. Or they could learn their way around a kitchen working in the cafeteria. They also help by collecting recyclables, watering plants, or feeding the fish in the school aquarium.

Typical Week's Menu

| Monday: Curried pork and rice |
| Tuesday: Meatballs and mashed potatoes |
| Wednesday: Fish with dill sauce and potatoes |
| Thursday: Pea soup and pancakes with jam |
| Friday: Chicken pasta |

After-School Activities

As the school day draws to a close, students put on their coats, grab their backpacks, and head on out, but few of them go home. At that hour, most Finnish parents are still at work, and spending the rest of the afternoon at home alone isn't much fun. The younger students are ushered out of the school to a nearby playground, where there's supervision and an afternoon snack.

For teens, there might be several hobby clubs that meet after school, but the activities vary by the school and region. Some head to soccer or hockey practice, while others set off to compete in a cross-country running or gymnastics meet. Some simply visit the pool to swim laps.

A Sporting Life

Finland has a long history of sports and fitness. More than 94 percent of Finns ages 19 to 65 report they exercise regularly, making the country one of the most physically active in the world.

Young people embrace exercise and sports more than any other age group. In one recent survey, 91 percent of children between 3 and 18 years old participated in sports on a regular basis.

Around 40 percent of all Finnish teens belong to an organized sports club or team. There are more than 7,800 sports clubs scattered throughout the country, many of them organized exclusively for the 800,000 young athletes who participate. The most popular sports among teens are soccer, cycling, cross-country skiing, badminton, Nordic walking, and running.

Among girls, the most popular sports are swimming and gymnastics. For boys, the favorite sports are soccer

Hockey has been a part of Finnish life for more than a century. In 1899 a game resembling hockey was first described in a Finnish sports magazine.

and floor ball—a sport that resembles hockey, but is played indoors without skates and with a ball instead of a puck.

Choosing the Future

By the time Finnish students turn 16, they have a choice to make. Some will choose to attend upper secondary school, or high school, to prepare for college. About half of all students earn a high school diploma; of those, about 60 percent are girls. The rest may choose a three year vocational school. Only around 6 percent of students choose to end their education at 16.

After students turn 18 years old, complete their high school work, and pass the matriculation exam—a standardized test designed to test students'

preparation for upper-level education—they are given a graduation certificate. Fewer than 7 percent of students failed their graduation exams in 2005.

The students who pass their exams attend a ceremony to receive a special certificate, a white cap, and a red rose. Boys often wear a suit or sport coat and tie; girls wear a simple spring dress. After the ceremony, students return home for a party with food, presents, and picture-taking.

More Schooling?

Finland's universities are public and supported by the government. There are 21 universities and colleges in Finland, with a total enrollment of more than 150,000 students.

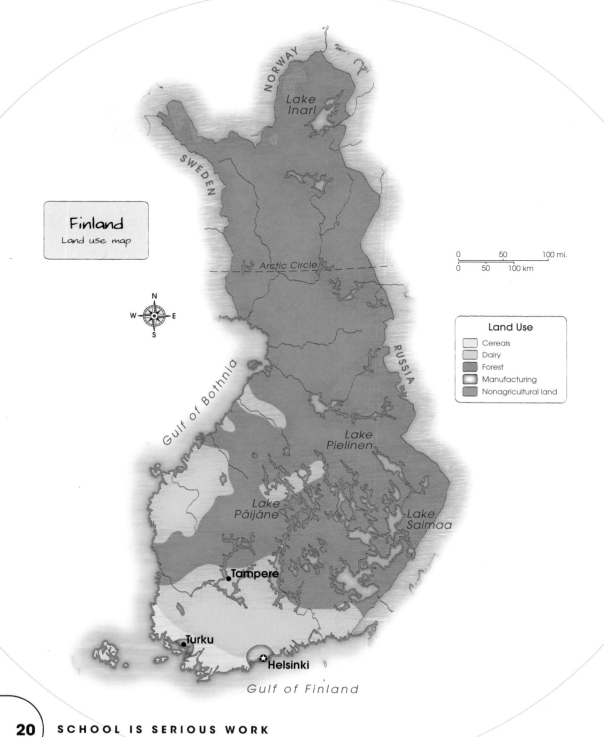

Finland
Land use map

Arctic Circle

Lake Inari

NORWAY

SWEDEN

RUSSIA

Gulf of Bothnia

Lake Pielinen

Lake Päijäne

Lake Saimaa

Tampere

Turku

Helsinki

Gulf of Finland

N
W E
S

0	50	100 mi.
0	50	100 km

Land Use
- Cereals
- Dairy
- Forest
- Manufacturing
- Nonagricultural land

The smallest schools in Finland have as few as 10 students. The largest have more than 900.

Other students opt for two years of technical training for a career. Recently those taking the technical path also have been allowed to take the university exam after their studies. There are technical schools, or polytechnics, which provide instruction in industries like technology, tourism, and education, and in business administration. These schools are privately owned but receive 57 percent of their funding from the government. About 114,000 students attend 29 polytechnics in the country.

Entrance to Finland's universities is based on a point system. Those with the best grades in high school earn the most points. However, that is not always enough to get into the school they want. Each university has its own entrance exam, and scoring well on that test usually means more to the university than actual school grades.

Overall, there are 20 degree programs for Finnish students to choose from. The most popular programs include technology, humanities, and natural sciences, while less popular programs include theater and dance, veterinary medicine, and art and creative design. Language and communications courses are mandatory, regardless of the program chosen.

The average university student attends seven or eight years of college before earning a degree. Because Finland's universities are so affordable, many students attend for years after earning their basic degree, studying for master's or doctoral degrees.

Finnish people are among the most frequent users of cell phones in the world. Nearly 80 percent of all Finns have at least one cell phone.

CHAPTER TWO

Finnish Daily Life

LIKE MANY OF THE HOMES IN SCANDINAVIA, Finnish homes are simple and clean in their design and decoration. They usually have white or cream-colored walls adorned with just a few special pieces of art or photography. There has been a recent trend of adding impressive modern touches, like home theaters and spas with indoor saunas.

Storage space is usually built-in cupboards or bookshelves, trimmed in light wood. Furniture, also light-colored, often includes a leather chair and a simple but comfortable sofa. Side tables, coffee tables, and knickknacks are kept to a minimum.

Floors are generally a plain, light wood, with a few rugs in entryways or hallways. Few Finnish apartments or houses have carpeting. Finns worry about being able to properly clean carpeting, so they usually avoid it. It is also customary for people to remove their shoes when entering a home—both to protect the shiny wood floors and to avoid tracking snow, dirt, and mud in the house from the outside.

Some have suggested this rather simple style is

Finland's three strongest industries—forestry and wood-related products, electronics, and metalworks—have made a huge impact on Finnish design.

influenced by the Lutheran faith, the country's dominant religion. Lutherans generally stress modesty and humility, which may carry over into the way Finns decorate their homes. Another reason for this design could simply be that it is a classic look that is appreciated by many people.

Modern Finnish homes are highly energy-efficient. Cold winters and

Toiling at Chores and Jobs

Since Finns rarely rely on others to help clean their houses, chores are typically shared among the parents and children of the house. Teens are expected to pitch in by setting the table, washing dishes, taking out garbage, collecting and sorting items for recycling, or mowing the lawn.

Mothers still do most of the cooking and cleaning in the typical Finnish house. More men are taking on those jobs, though, especially as an increasing number of women are pursuing careers of their own. In recent years, more men have decided to stay home to take care of the children and tend to the house.

Since the government has imposed strict rules about teens' working outside the house, most Finnish teens earn a small allowance of about 10 euros (U.S.$14.20) for helping out with household chores. They use the extra pocket money for buying CDs, snacks, magazines, or going to movies.

Munching and Mealtime

For Finnish teens, food is as much about nutrition and energy as it is about enjoyment. During the long, cold winters, they burn a lot of calories just staying warm. In the summer, many teens play sports and stay active, so they need a healthful and balanced diet then, too.

The biggest family meal of the day used to be lunchtime, but breakfast has become the main meal at which the family dines together during the week.

warm summers make it a challenge to heat and cool houses. Houses are often well-insulated and have heavy, thick windows to keep out the cold or hot air, depending on the season.

On weekends, families savor a large meal together around 2 P.M., but during the week, busy school, work, and activity schedules make it hard for Finnish families to gather for lunch—and even for dinner. So in the early morning, they have their first meal of the day together. The breakfast menu might include porridge, bran, müesli (a granolalike cereal), yogurt, milk, and *ruisleipä*, or rye bread.

ruisleipa
(rui-is-LAY-pah)

There are also fresh berries and fruit juice on the table. Teens are also fans of boxed cereals. Recently many Finnish families have started choosing a dark-roasted coffee in the morning instead of the traditional light-roasted blend.

Finnish dinners are traditionally prepared at home from basic ingredients. Casseroles and soups are common in western Finland, while mushroom dishes, pies, and a special meat dish called Karelian stew are more common in the east.

The Finnish diet is one of balance and moderation. Meals are often prepared from scratch, but prepackaged or even fast foods are becoming more common as families become busier and busier.

makkara
(muck-karah)

A Finnish sausage, called *makkara*, has always been a favorite. Sometimes it is even called the Finnish fast food. Usually grilled and eaten with mustard, it is served at many meals and is featured at festivals, concerts, and celebrations. As one old Finnish saying goes, "A Finn is never too full to eat a bit more sausage."

The cuisine of Finland is well known for the use of whole-grain products like rye, barley, and oats. Finland is the northernmost grower of bread grains in the world, and the average Finn eats 110 pounds (50 kg) of bread a year.

The Finnish diet has grown more healthful in the past few decades. Today there are more organic foods—which are grown without harsh chemicals—and grocery stores offer more foods with reduced fat and calories.

Bread is served during all meals. Casseroles, meatballs or meatloaf, and fish are typical everyday food. Pasta, rice, and potatoes are common side dishes. And *makaroonilaatikko*, a macaroni casserole made with hamburger, vegetables, eggs, milk, and butter, is always a popular choice.

In the country, a typical lunch includes regional specialties like filled dumplings called pirogi, *kalakukko*, which is fish baked in rye bread, or a savory pastry called Karelian pie. The pie is made with a thin rye crust filled with rice and eaten with butter mixed with boiled eggs.

makaroonilaatikko
(muck-AH-rohn-il-ah-tikk-OH)
kalakukko
(KALL-ah-KUKK-oh)

For city dwellers, lunch might include sausage, meatballs, or a salmon or cabbage casserole. But it

Coffee Culture

Coffee is an important part of daily Finnish life. In fact, it is considered the national drink. It is served during most meals and celebrations. Most workplaces have at least two coffee breaks during the day. In the early 1800s, coffee was a luxury and only consumed by the rich. As it became less expensive, Finns everywhere adopted the hot drink. Today serving coffee is expected when entertaining guests, even during the most casual visit. Scandinavians have the highest rate of coffee consumption in the world—the average Finn drinks four or more cups of coffee a day, or more than 1,400 cups a year!

Make it With Milk

Not only is milk a favorite beverage with many Finnish meals, but it is also an ingredient in many traditional dishes. There are meals made with milk that is curdled, soured, or cultured. Milk makes a regular appearance in broths, soups, stews, and puddings. A regional favorite, *leipäjuusto*, or squeaky cheese, is fresh cheese traditionally made from cow's beestings, also known as colostrum, which is the first milk a cow gives after calving.

leipäjuusto
(lae-pa-you-sto)

could just as likely be an Asian stir fry, Indian tandoori, tacos, pastas, soups, or a salad.

So where does all that food come from? Finland has traditional grocery stores and supermarkets, but in the spring, summer, and fall, many Finnish families rely on large outdoor markets for their fresh produce, meat, and poultry. Visiting the markets is often a family affair, with everybody choosing their seasonal favorites. They bring tote bags or carts to carry their purchases home, usually buying enough food to last them the rest of the week. The shopping carts are filled with a selection of cold meats, yogurt, milk, cheese, bread, and potatoes.

Though Finns enjoy home cooking, families are opting to dine out more often as their schedules grow busier. Italian cuisine is popular, and pizza is a particular favorite among teens. In bigger cities, restaurant menus offer a long list of international dishes. Russian food has been a staple of Finnish dining for decades. Today Japanese and Mexican restaurants are popping up in many parts of the country, as families experiment with fresh new tastes and modern culinary trends.

For teens, fast food is always a favorite. McDonald's restaurants abound in Finland. There teens can order a burger on rye, called a McRye (or McRuis in Finnish). Yet the Finns have their own answer to McDonald's: Hesburger, a homegrown burger chain

In 2007, Finland banned smoking in bars and restaurants. More than 80 percent of Finns agreed with the ban, a higher number than in any other country.

beloved by young Finns everywhere. The chain has enjoyed a great deal of success. In 1992, there were only 12 stores in operation. By 2007, there were more than 200 Hesburger restaurants in Finland, Estonia, Germany, and Latvia, serving 100,000 customers a day.

Clothing: Finnish With Style

Finland has become a growing force in international fashion, thanks to cities like Helsinki, where a number of designers have set up shop. Like Paris, Milan, and New York, Helsinki hosts its own Fashion Week, when clothing designers showcase their latest creations on beautiful models who stroll down the catwalk. Finnish style favors simple designs made of high-quality fabrics. Many teens take advantage of the fashion trends, flooding boutiques, stores, and malls to snatch up designer T-shirts, jeans, and dresses.

Katariina Rauko, a 15-year-old girl in Helsinki, said she and her friends have really different styles:

Some follow trends and some like very personal clothes and some don't care at all about style. For me, fashion is a passion.

For the most part, however, Finns prefer casual clothes to formal dresses,

suits, or ties. Part of the reason is the weather. It is not always practical to dress for the cold while wearing formal clothes. Even business managers tend to dress "city casual," which is usually a dress shirt, sweater, and plain slacks for men or dress slacks and a sweater or long-sleeved shirt for women.

There are no uniforms at any of Finland's public schools, and students are free to wear whatever they want— within reason. Girls are more inclined to wear pants or jeans than skirts or dresses. They might wear tank tops or a frilly shirt in the warmer months. Boys are most often spotted wearing jeans, T-shirts, sweatshirts, and athletic jerseys.

Although Finnish styles are gaining in popularity, teens' fashion choices are also influenced by styles from the United States, Japan, and other parts of Europe.

Finnish clothing is quite colorful, especially the clothing worn during the long winter months. Stripes of red, green, blue, and yellow often accent knit sweaters, caps, scarves, and mittens. Even warm jackets boast bright colors. Children stay snug in one-piece snowsuits, bundled against the cold for long periods of outdoor play.

Finns do not stay indoors in winter. They prefer to be outside—almost as much as they do in summer. From a young age, children frolic outside in all weather. As the old Finnish saying goes, "There's no such thing as bad weather, only bad clothing."

City Life, Rural Life

Most people in Finland live in cities. Helsinki, the nation's capital, is the largest city and is home to about one-sixth of the country's more than 5 million citizens.

That was not always the case. Before the 1950s, almost 75 percent of Finns lived and worked in rural areas, tending to their farms. As farming became more automated with the use of machinery, there was less need for family farms. Families gradually left their land in search of a new life in the cities. Now 62 percent of Finns live in cities, and 38 percent live and work in rural areas.

Plenty of coffee, sauna time, warm clothing, and outdoor activities help Finns get through the winter.

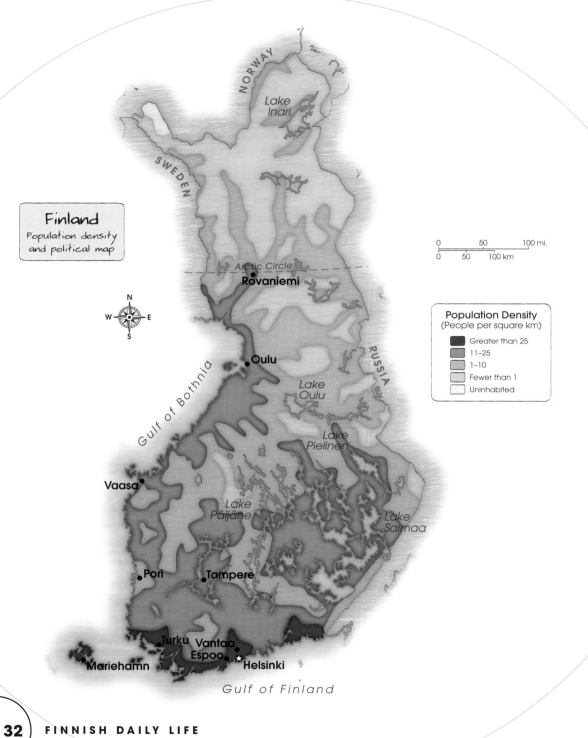

Finland

Population density
and political map

NORWAY

Lake
Inari

SWEDEN

RUSSIA

Arctic Circle
Rovaniemi

N
W · E
S

Oulu

Lake
Oulu

Gulf of Bothnia

Lake
Pielinen

Vaasa

Lake
Päijäne

Lake
Saimaa

Pori   **Tampere**

Turku   **Vantaa**
Espoo
Mariehamn   ☆ **Helsinki**

Gulf of Finland

0   50   100 mi.
0   50   100 km

Population Density
(People per square km)

■ Greater than 25
■ 11–25
■ 1–10
□ Fewer than 1
□ Uninhabited

In Finland's largest cities, most families live in apartments or town-homes. Single-family dwellings usually lie farther from the city center. Most apartments are two- and three-bedroom units, big enough to accommodate the average family with two children.

Finland has a well-developed transportation system. Because of this, many people choose public transportation, and only half of the population owns a car. Most families get by with just one car, which is used by one or both parents to get to work and to take children to and from school. Families without a car rely on Finland's bus and train system to get around. Boats, taxis, and airplanes are also available.

In Helsinki, streets and sidewalks are filled with commuters, shoppers, and tourists. Finns work in gleaming office buildings, shop in designer boutiques, and go skating in the central square. In the evenings, teens head

Coffee is seen as a social drink in Finland, and coffee shops are a popular hangout. Finns drink 23 pounds (10.4 kg) of coffee per person every year.

downtown to dance at the many clubs, catch a cutting-edge independent film, or hang out in a cafe sipping coffee and chatting with friends.

For those who live in the country, farmhouses and cottages are the typical home styles. They are usually made of stone or wood, and have wooden shingles and a fireplace.

On the farm, men, women, and teens each have special jobs. The women tend to the cattle and other livestock. They also are in charge of taking care of the children, making meals, cleaning the barn and the house, and entertaining guests. The men are responsible for taking care of the pastures and hayfields, cutting wood, operating machinery, and working with other farmers so that there is enough help during the harvest. Teens are often asked to help feed the animals, milk cows,

Reindeer herding has been important to the Sami, the indigenous people of Finland. Today around 900 Sami families and other families earn a living by reindeer herding.

clean animal stalls, bale hay, or gather the harvest.

At the end of a long day of school and chores, a Finnish teen is apt to sit in a sauna, take a dip in a nearby lake or stream, or relax and read by the fire at night. If they have friends nearby, they might meet to play games or drive to the nearest town in search of fun.

Picking berries or wild mushrooms is a popular pastime in the summer. According to Finland's traditional "rights of common access," everyone has the right to pick wild produce, no matter who owns the land. Every year, around

88 million pounds (40 million kg) of berries and 13.2 million pounds (6 million kg) of mushrooms are collected. Thousands of foreign berry pickers gather in Finland every year. Most pickers come from Thailand, Ukraine, Mongolia, and Japan, and spend around 10 weeks gathering blueberries, lingonberries, and other Finnish delicacies.

For centuries, it was customary for men to leave their farms to their children, who, in turn, were expected to work the land and care for their aging parents. Now many of those offspring

Cleanliness

One of the most striking things about Finland is how clean most of it is. Even the biggest cities seem spotless. There is almost no litter or garbage on the streets or sidewalks. Finns take great pride in keeping things neat and tidy in their homes, and this attitude seems to extend to public areas as well. There are strict recycling laws, and Finland has a

very impressive recycling rate of nearly 99 percent for refillable bottles. Risto Saarinen, director of the Federation of the Brewing and Soft Drinks Industry, said:

Finland's recycling rate is among the highest in the world, and as a result, refillable bottles are the environmentally friendliest form of packaging for beverages.

Finnish winters are extreme. In 2006, the temperatures were so low that electricity use skyrocketed to record levels.

are opting to leave farming altogether. Those who inherit the family farm and choose to work it are expected to give a portion of the proceeds to siblings who gave up their share of the land.

Today more women than men are leaving the farms and choosing to live in cities. The trend has left many bachelor farmers going it alone or relying on other young men, instead of families, to work their farms.

Cold and Hot Climates

The weather in Finland swings from one extreme to another over the course of a year. Winters are long, dark, and cold. Summers are sunny and warm.

In the winter, days are short, especially in the far north, where daylight can last just a few hours at most. Above the Arctic Circle, the polar night lasts 51 days. During this time, the sun never rises above the horizon.

Winter daytime highs average around 16 degrees Fahrenheit (minus 9 degrees Celsius) in January and February, which are the coldest months. Overnight low temperatures dip down to minus 58 F (minus 50 C) in the northern regions. And there is snow—lots of snow. In a typical winter, Finland can have as much as 3 feet (90 centimeters) of snow on the ground.

In the summer, it is the opposite. In

the far north, the polar day causes the sun to stay above the horizon, making for long summer days that are good for farming. Summer temperatures can reach 95 F (35 C) in the interior and southern portions of the country.

Geography and Regions

Finland is a country of trees and water. Throughout the country, dense forests grow along gleaming lakes, ponds, and rivers. Nearly 70 percent of Finland is covered by forests, and there are more than 188,000 lakes.

With so much of the country covered with forests and water, only 8 percent of Finland's countryside is suitable for farming.

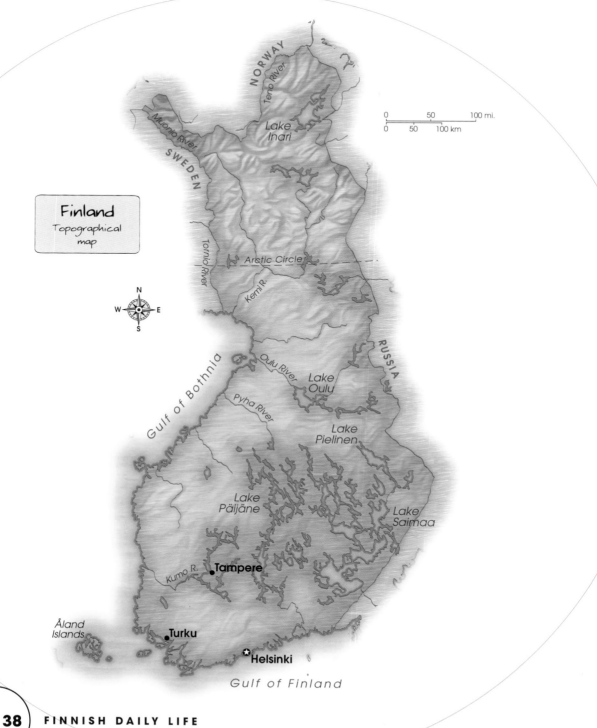

Finland
Topographical
map

NORWAY

Teno River

Muonio River

SWEDEN

Lake
Inari

0   50   100 mi.
0   50   100 km

Tornio River

Arctic Circle

N
W · E
S

Kemi R.

Gulf of Bothnia

Oulu River

Lake
Oulu

RUSSIA

Pyha River

Lake
Pielinen

Lake
Päijäne

Lake
Saimaa

Kumo R.

●Tampere

Åland
Islands

●Turku

✪ Helsinki

Gulf of Finland

Key characteristics of several regions affect how Finns live in them. In the southern region, the climate is more temperate, meaning the temperatures do not rise or fall as much as they do in the northern regions. The waters of the Gulf of Bothnia to the west and the Baltic Sea and Gulf of Finland to the south help moderate temperatures in the southern half of Finland during much of the year.

Farming is largely limited to the southern and western portions of the country where topsoil is fertile and the days are warm enough to raise crops. Livestock farming, especially dairy farming, is often the only form of profitable farming in the rest of the country.

One-quarter of Finland lies above the Arctic Circle, where few Finns live. Winters there are long, cold, and harsh, with little sunlight. The landscape is

The Chapel of Ice in Helsinki is a popular location for winter weddings. It is one of several ice buildings constructed in Finland's winter months. However, with the onset of global warming, the winters aren't always cold enough to build the chapel.

39

largely snow-covered, but the summer sun can reveal rocky terrain, hardy grasslands, and dwarf shrubs.

Finland's diverse climate yields a variety of habitats for plants and animals. Finland is home to more than 42,000 species of plants, animals, and

fungi. Reindeer, elk, and deer scour the forest floor and nibble on small plants. Brown bears, lynx, wolves, and wolverines prowl the forests for prey. Golden eagles soar and circle overhead in search of small mammals. Seals thrive in the Saimaa lakes, a chain of lakes and waterways in the southeastern part of Finland. It is the largest lake system

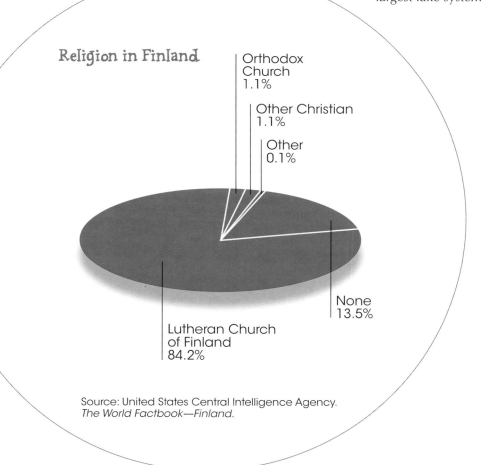

Religion in Finland

Orthodox Church 1.1%

Other Christian 1.1%

Other 0.1%

None 13.5%

Lutheran Church of Finland 84.2%

Source: United States Central Intelligence Agency. *The World Factbook—Finland.*

The Importance of Being Confirmed

Around 90 percent of Finnish children are baptized at birth, and teens are encouraged to receive confirmation as members of the Lutheran church when they turn 15. About 90 percent of them attend confirmation classes. Most attend confirmation summer camps in beautiful, natural locations. Public schools also offer religious education in the student's particular religion, though only for those who wish to participate. Alternative courses on moral philosophy are also sometimes available.

in the country at 1,690 square miles (4,394 sq km). It includes 14,000 islands. Lake Saimaa, the largest lake in Finland and fourth largest in Europe, is part of this aquatic chain.

Religion and Worship

Churches with tall, pointed steeples are common in Finland. They dot the countryside and squeeze in next to other buildings in larger cities. With more than 80 percent of Finns considering themselves Lutherans, the country holds firm to its long Christian tradition.

The outside of most Lutheran churches is elegantly decorated with intricate stone or woodwork. These churches come in many styles, from simple wood to elegant and striking modern designs. Inside there is usually a pipe organ for playing hymns, pews to sit in, and a pulpit for the pastor to address the congregation.

In spite of the number of churches, many of them are sparsely attended on Sunday mornings. While Finns say they respect the church and Lutheran beliefs, many worship at home or pray privately. About 6 percent of Finns attend church once a month; half go just once a year. Christmas Eve is the most popular day for Finns to attend church, causing many churches to have standing room only for services that day.

Although couples may live together for several years and even have children, they are marrying later in life. The average age for Finnish brides is 30 and grooms are often close to 32.

3

Fun With Friends & Family

FROM AN EARLY AGE, FINNISH CHILDREN ARE ENCOURAGED TO FIND FRIENDS AND PLAYMATES and develop a sense of independence. Both parents are usually at work when the school day ends, so teens are forced to entertain themselves. Kaisa Pakarinen, a 13-year-old girl in Helsinki, said:

After school, I play computer games, play piano or go out with my friends. When I hang out with my friends, we like talking, romping, and laughing.

Some schools offer teens a variety of after-school activities, including sports, art, music, and acting classes. If they are not busy with an organized event, teens may hang out with their friends at coffee shops, malls, and video game arcades.

Chances are good they are also going out on dates. Every family has its own rules for dating, but Finns are not strict about what age is most appropriate. Some Finns start dating in their early teens, and most begin by the time they turn 14 or 15. Classmates gather for group dates at the ice rink or ski hill. Boys and girls might pair off to see a movie or hang out at the mall.

They often bring dates to parties and listen to music.

When real courtship begins, young men are usually quite considerate of their female companions. They hold the door open for them, help them with their coats, and stand when they enter a room. They might not, however, express their appreciation or love with words. Finns are generally reserved with their feelings. As one old joke goes, a Finnish woman was asking her husband of 40 years if he still loved her. He replied, "Sweetie, I told you I loved you 40 years ago. If anything changes, I'll let you know." Teens are beginning to open up as other languages allow a more casual tone: "I love you" sounds much less serious than "Minä rakastan sinua"!

While friendships and independence are important, families remain an important part of a Finnish teen's life. Many teens continue to enjoy spending time with their parents and

Minä rakastan sinua
(Min-AH rakastan SIH-nua)

Single-parent households are becoming more common in Finland. However, fewer than 3 percent of all families are headed by fathers only.

The social security offered by the country makes it easy for young people to get a good start in life.

siblings throughout adolescence. They play games and sports together, take long camping or snowmobiling trips, or travel overseas. They also might stay with their parents in cabins during the summer, or at least visit the cabins with their friends for a weekend.

Most Finnish families have two children; families with three children are the next most common. About one-fifth of Finnish families have only one child. When more Finns were farmers and needed extra help, families were considerably larger—with four, five, and even six children. Now that more families live in cities, smaller families have become more standard. People are also getting married at an older age—often in their early 30s—so there is less time to have children.

Finnish children leave home to live on their own between the ages of 18 and 20, either to attend college or begin a career. As the population grows older on average, more households are without children. Almost a quarter of

Finnish homes are childless. One reason for this is that women are becoming more educated than men, and decide to wait longer to have children or not to have them at all.

Births and Names

When Finnish couples marry, the woman usually takes the man's last name. However, more Finnish women are choosing to keep the names they grew up with. In 1986, the law made it possible for a woman to keep her maiden name and gave the husband the right to take his wife's name, combine their names to make a marital double name, or create a completely new identity.

Nearly all Finnish children are born in hospitals, especially if the parents live in a city. Rural children might be born at home, often with the help of a midwife, but this is extremely rare. When this happens, mother and child may be taken to the

Most Popular Baby Names

Boys	Girls
Johannes	Emilia
Matias	Olivia
Aleksi	Katariina
Antero	Amanda
Tapani	Matilda
Samuel	Emma
Emil	Iida
Leevi	Ella
Rasmus	Aada
Ville	Karoliina

Source: *Babycenter.com (May 2007)*

hospital for a checkup after the delivery or if there are complications.

Elderly Living

It is also rare for three generations of Finns to live together. In fact, few children decide to live near their parents once they move out of the house, as a form of independence and adulthood. That makes it difficult for adult children to help care for their older parents and can make aging a lonely experience.

Most senior citizens continue living in their own homes long after they have retired. Support from the government makes aging an easier burden to bear. The government gives aid to the elderly so they can live at home for as long as they wish. For those who cannot live on their own, there are special retirement homes, hospitals, and communities. Such places give older Finns the health care they need and the comfort of belonging to a group or extended family. The average Finn retires at age 59; however, this age has been rising since a policy change in 2005 allowed workers under age 68 to continue their jobs. Nearly 1 million Finns, or 16 percent of the population, are 65 or older.

Pets

The Finnish family pet is most likely to be a dog, though cats are a close second. For Finns intent on honoring the national dog, the breed should be a Finnish spitz. The spitz is a native of Finland and was originally bred for hunting and barking to scare prey out of hiding. Most spitzes are caramel-colored and have pointed ears and slightly upturned mouths that make it look as if they are always smiling. Spitzes are loyal and protective, with excellent hearing, making them good watchdogs.

Finnish spitz have been used to hunt moose, elk, and even bear.

Crafts and Collecting

For centuries, Finns have taken pride in making things themselves. From homes to clothes to glassware, Finnish craftsmanship and handiwork have played an important role in preserving the culture.

Teens can take courses to learn skills that have been passed down for generations. Young people can learn how to make furniture, wooden baskets, and metalwork. For boys, crafting their first *puukko,* or sheath knife, can be a rite of passage to adulthood in some regions. For girls, sewing lace and weaving wall rugs, called *ryijy,*

puukko
(pu-koh)

ryijy
(ruy-yuu)

The puukko design is more than 1,000 years old, and the knife is a traditional tool of the Scandinavian people.

are traditional crafts they can learn if interested.

Finns are internationally recognized for their hobby of collecting. Stamps and coins have been the most popular items for collectors. Youngsters are especially eager to start collections. There are national stamp clubs, many with special sections for young collectors. Recently teens have been collecting long-distance telephone calling cards featuring portraits of famous people or colorful cartoons. Other collectables that attract teens are stuffed animals, toys, miniature cars, postcards, sports items, comic books, and magazines.

The Moomins

The Moomins are lumpy, lovable cartoon characters almost every Finn grows up enjoying. They were created in 1945 as part of a children's book by Tove Jansson. The characters sprang from a story about a little Moomintroll and his parents, Moominmomma and Moominpappa. The family lives in Moomin Valley, a mysterious and peaceful world. A series of novels and comic books led to a TV series that first aired in 1969. Since then there have been other TV specials and even an opera based on the Moomins. Moomin World in Naantali is one of the most visited tourist attractions in Finland.

The Moomin series has been translated into Swedish, German, Japanese, Russian, and English.

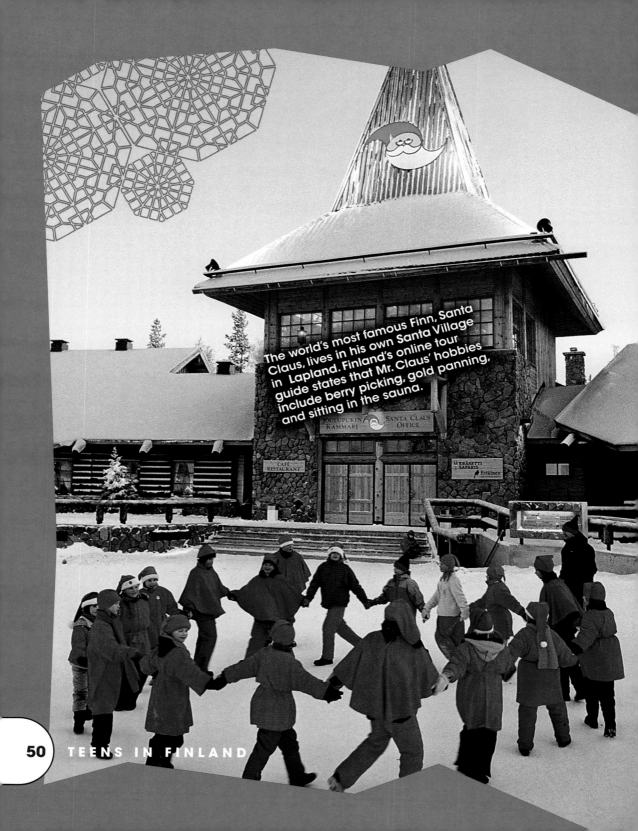

The world's most famous Finn, Santa Claus, lives in his own Santa Village in Lapland. Finland's online tour guide states that Mr. Claus' hobbies include berry picking, gold panning, and sitting in the sauna.

4

Party Time & Celebrations

TO A FINNISH CHILD, HIS OR HER BIRTHDAY IS ABOUT THE BEST DAY OF THE YEAR. It is also an important day for the family.

Parties are held on either a Saturday or Sunday so that the entire family can attend. Grandmas, grandpas, aunts, uncles, and cousins show up with gifts and good wishes. The birthday child is considered a "hero" for the day and is greeted with the Finnish phrase "Onneksi Olkoon!", or "To your happiness!" Guests sing "Happy Birthday" the moment they walk in the door. Finnish tradition dictates that children get to open their birthday presents as soon as they are received.

Birthday meals are served around lunchtime. There are salads and sausages and—for a summer party—a glass of *sima*, a traditional May Day drink, or Finnish soda, berry juice, or, for adults, a glass of beer or wine.

Dessert is the customary Finnish birthday cake. It's

Onneksi Olkoon
(on-nexih awl-corn)
sima
(see-ma)

made in three layers and filled with strawberries, bananas, and whipped cream. The cake is topped with more whipped cream, fruit, and candies—and then a candle for each year of the child's life.

Onginta
(oon-gin-tah)

Before everyone leaves, the children take turns playing *onginta*, which means "fishing" in Finnish. Adults hold up a cloth or sheet, and children are given a fishing rod with a line attached. They dangle the line over the side of the sheet, where an adult attaches a small basket of prizes. When they pull up their line, the children get to see what they caught.

Christmas Tops All Holidays

Churches are packed, presents are wrapped, and Santa Claus is on his way! It is Jouluaatto, or Christmas Eve, and Finns are eager to celebrate their favorite holiday.

Families gather in their homes to open presents, sing carols, and share a large, traditional meal. Favorite Christmas foods include salted salmon,

Although Finns have quite an array of sweets to choose from, fruit is usually a main ingredient.

A Calendar of Finnish Holidays

Uudenvuodenpäivä (New Year's Day)—January 1

Loppiainen (Epiphany)—January 6

Runebergin päivä (Runeberg's Day)—February 5

Pääsiäispäivä (Easter, including Easter Monday)—March/April

Vappu (May Day)—May 1

Helatorstai (Ascension Day)—May

Whitsun (Pentecost)—May/June

Juhannusaatto and Juhannuspäivä (Midsummer holidays)—Third weekend in June

Pyhäinpäivä (All Saints' Day)—November 1

Itsenäisyyspäivä (Independence Day)—December 6

Jouluaatto (Christmas Eve)—December 24

Joulupäivä (Christmas Day)—December 25

Tapaninpäivä (St. Stephen's Day or Boxing Day)—December 26

caviar (fish eggs), baked lutefisk (a salty fish soaked in lye), salads, casseroles, rice porridge, liver paté, mixed fruit soup, bread, cookies, and other desserts.

A typical Christmas Eve meal includes spiced wine, baked ham, mashed potatoes, berry sauces and jellies, and applesauce.

Dessert is often sweet puffed-pastry pinwheels stuffed with prunes, spicy gingerbread cookies, or sugar-cinnamon spiced rice porridge with a whole almond hidden in it. The one who finds the almond receives a special gift or gets to make a wish that will supposedly come true during the new year.

Santa receives more than 700,000 letters a year at his address in Finland.

Santa's Workshop

Santa Claus has a history almost as old as Finland itself. In fact, Finns claim their country is the home of Father Christmas. Santa is called Joulupukki, which means "Yule goat" or "Christmas goat." The name has been traced to an old tradition in which people dressed in goat hides, and a fabled ghost, called a *nuuttipukki*, wandered from house to house, eating leftover Christmas food. Today Santa Claus lives in Lapland in a village near Rovaniemi, at the Arctic Circle. He has a shop where local Lapps help him craft colorful handmade gifts and an area where visitors can see his team of reindeer between November and January.

nuuttipukki
(nu-ut-tih-puk-kih)

Since a large portion of Finland lies within the Arctic Circle, it is no surprise that Santa Claus is a big part of every Christmas. After all, Santa is only a short sleigh ride away!

Other Holidays

Itsenäisyyspäivä, or Independence Day, is another favorite Finnish holiday. Observed every December 6, the day marks Finland's independence from Russia in 1917. Usually Finns gather for a large lunch with family members at a restaurant. In the evenings, they go home and place candles in the windows. Then they turn on the television and watch a live broadcast of a reception held by the president of Finland. Famous and important Finns are invited to the gala. Although traditionally a somber event, the holiday has recently become more lively, with celebrations, fireworks, and parades.

Runebergin päivä, or Runeberg's Day, is named for the poet Johan Ludvig Runeberg. Also known as National Poet's Day, it is not an official government holiday, so nobody gets a day off from work or school. Still, every February 5, families place a lit candle in their windows and gather to eat a piece of Runeberg's Tart, a small, round sponge cake seasoned with almonds and rum and decorated with raspberry jam and a sugar ring.

A popular holiday among teens and young children is Pääsiäispäivä, or Easter, which falls in March or April.

The tradition is for children to dress in costumes and go from house to house in their neighborhood, collecting candy and other treats.

Girls may dress as good witches wearing shawls and holding pussy willow branches decorated with pink and yellow feathers. They ring doorbells and shout, "Please give us coins or candy!" or recite poems of good luck. During the night, the Easter rooster delivers eggs to children while they are sleeping, and they awake to baskets of goodies.

Parents hide chocolate eggs in their gardens for children to find on Easter.

Vappu, or May Day, begins on the eve of April 30, which is also International Labor Day. May Day is a very carnivallike celebration. People don the white caps they wore at graduation, put up decorations, and enjoy a day away from work—eating, drinking, and having informal parties with friends and family.

Juhannusaatto, or Midsummer, is another exciting time. Held on the third weekend in June, the holiday marks the longest days of the year. Finns everywhere leave the cities to spend time in the country. At most Midsummer festivals around the country, there is music, dancing, food, and an enormous bonfire.

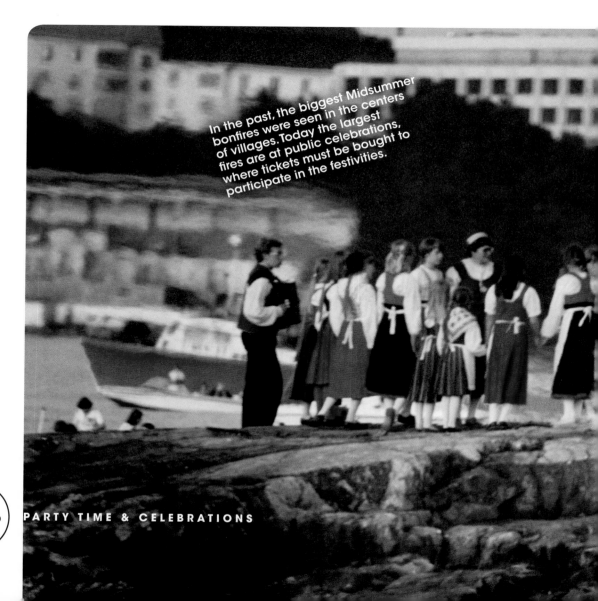

In the past, the biggest Midsummer bonfires were seen in the centers of villages. Today the largest fires are at public celebrations, where tickets must be bought to participate in the festivities.

On Uudenvuodenpäivä, or New Year's Eve, Finns celebrate with fireworks, songs, and resolutions.

Singing, dancing, and eating are central to most Finnish festivals, and there are hundreds of such celebrations during the year.

The biggest festivals focus on music, and include the Savonlinna

Opera Festival, the Kaustinen Folk Music Festival, the Kuhmo Chamber Music Festival, Pori Jazz, Turku Ruisrock, and the Joensuu Song Festival. Concerts featuring jazz, blues, and rock music are held in many places during the summer. The largest are in Oulu, Seinajoki, and Pihtipudas, where performers such as Bob Dylan, Billy Idol, and R.E.M. have attracted 25,000 to 30,000 fans. Finland Festivals, an organization responsible for planning cultural events, has brought 20,000 performing artists to more than 2 million concertgoers. An annual dance and music celebration in Kuopio attracts performers and fans from around the world.

Young people play a pivotal role in Finnish festivals as participants, performers, and employees. Teens are as likely to be found dancing onstage as they are standing behind the counter at a food tent. They also help clean and pack up when the day draws to a close.

Finnish National Costume

Wearing the Finnish national costume for special events remains a strong tradition among both urban and rural Finns. It is a standard feature at any of the many festivals during the year. While there are about 500 patterns, styles, and variations on the colorful outfits, there are some common features.

For women, the costume usually includes a smock, a colorful plaid or print skirt, a bodice or kirtle, a plain white apron, a jacket, a white head-

Costumes today are copies of clothing from the 18th and 19th centuries.

women wear are knitted from sheer linen or wool, and are held up by garters. Footwear varies and can include leather shoes with laces or buckles, or moccasins.

While most often worn at festivals, the national costume can also be spotted at special occasions such as weddings, graduations, concerts, or folk dance performances. Sometimes Finns wear only part of the costume—a hat, shoes, or jewelry, perhaps—while the rest of their outfit is modern.

Most of the costumes are handmade, according to family tradition passed down for generations. Adolescent Finnish boys and girls sometimes learn how to cut and sew their first costumes from their parents or grandparents.

A Wedding and a Funeral

On warm spring and summer evenings, a ritual is repeated in many parts of Finland. A young woman or man is led through the streets wearing a mask, offering odd bits of wisdom or performing silly tasks for complete strangers. They are brides- or grooms-to-be, participating in a growing pre-wedding custom.

Once limited to a few small villages, the tradition of Polttarit has grown popular throughout Finland. Separate parties for the bride and groom are held, a farewell to youth and a wild send-off into married life. Known around the world as stag or hen parties, Polttarit

dress, shoes, and kneesocks. Typical women's accessories include jewelry, belts, handkerchiefs, and a purse. For men, the costume consists of a shirt, dark trousers or knickers, a waistcoat, jacket, or coat, a hat or cap, a scarf, kneesocks, and shoes.

The kneesocks that men and

celebrations can become quite elaborate, depending on the friends throwing the party.

While weddings mark the formal start of a couple's life together, most Finnish couples have already lived together for several years before they get married. Many already have had children, and the children often become a part of the ceremony as attendants for their parents.

When the wedding day approaches, the festivities become more formal. Finnish weddings have become fancier and more expensive in the last few decades, but the size and style of weddings vary, depending on the couple. Urban professional couples seek more lavish, elaborate weddings, while rural couples tend to have less

Summertime is the most popular season for Finns to marry.

formal unions that concentrate on regional tradition.

Less conventional weddings may take place in the world's largest snow castle, in northern Finland, or in a chapel in a shopping mall. Most Finns, though, follow tradition when getting married. The majority of weddings are still held in churches and attended by friends and family members. Brides wear long white gowns and a veil, while grooms dress in tuxedos with tails.

Traditionally the bride's family was responsible for arranging and paying for the wedding. Today couples share the costs and planning associated with their own wedding. A large reception,

with music, dinner, dancing, and a wedding cake, follows the ceremony. Guests shower the bride and groom with presents.

Since 2002, same-sex marriages have been recognized. Finland was the last of the Scandinavian countries to accept the unions as legal, and by 2006, more than 950 same-sex couples were officially registered.

Funerals are usually held in a church and presided over by a member of the clergy. Finns are most often buried in a cemetery with a simple tombstone marking their grave. Most funerals are Lutheran, and nearly 98 percent of all funerals take place in a church.

Divorce

Even the fanciest wedding does not guarantee a happy or lasting marriage. Finland's divorce rates are among the highest in Europe. The Marriage Act, passed in 1988, made divorce much easier, which could have led to the higher rate of divorce. In fact, the annual divorce rate increased by nearly 150 percent after the act passed. Nevertheless, about two-thirds of Finnish families are headed by married couples.

Finnish graves are very well cared for by the family of the deceased or members of the church.

It is customary to take pictures of funerals or even videotape them. To Finns, death is a part of the cycle of life, and a funeral is another special occasion worth remembering. In fact, during All Hallow's Eve and Christmas Eve, cemeteries are known as *valomeri*, or seas of light. Finns visit cemeteries and light candles in remembrance of the deceased.

valomeri
(va-LOH-merri)

Helsinki's Market Square is a popular location to sell products to tourists and natives alike.

5

The World of Work

FOR THOSE UNDER 18, THERE ARE STRICT LAWS ABOUT WORK. Teens can only work during school vacations and in the evenings or on weekends. When they turn 14, they can work at a part-time job, but only for a few hours a week and only if it is light work that will not affect their health and well-being. They are supposed to devote most of their time to their studies.

When they turn 15, they can go to work full time if they have completed their required schooling. The law says they can decide how to spend the money they earn, even if they have not turned 18 and are still living with their parents.

Summer is the ideal time to find a job. Working at a summer camp and being part of a festival crew are some of the most popular jobs. At summer camp, teens might serve as counselors to younger children or help with meals and chores. At a festival, they might be called upon to set up tents and stages, prepare and sell food and clean things up when the day is done. Others might clean hotel rooms, deliver newspapers, or work as lifeguards at the many beaches.

Standing at Attention

When a Finnish boy turns 18, he is required to sign up for military service. All Finnish men under the age of 30 must register for military service, even in peacetime. Service can last for 170, 180, or 362 days, and more than 80 percent of men complete their time. Finnish men can be called upon to serve in wartime from ages 18 to 60. Nonmilitary service is also an option, and it includes training and work that benefits society. However, this alternative service must be approved. Women can apply for voluntary military service at age 18.

At 18, Finns are legally considered adults. They can vote in elections if they are Finnish citizens and have lived in the country for at least two years before the election. At 18, they can also apply for a passport without their parents, enter a bar for a drink, buy tobacco, or get married.

Politically Active and Aware

Finland's high standard of equality ensures that teens can hold political rallies, make speeches, write letters, and debate issues with everyone from their friends to their parents and some teachers. Some are politically active.

There are several formal organizations that either represent youth interests or give young people a platform to tackle larger projects. Nationally, more than 800,000 teens belong to youth organizations, many with a political purpose. Among the most popular and powerful are Left Youth, Socialdemocratic Youth of Finland, Student Union of the Centre Party, Youth League of the Coalition Party, and Finnish Christian Union Youth.

Teen girls have an especially potent role model in their president. In 2000, Tarja Halonen became the first female president of Finland. Re-elected in 2006, Halonen is a Social Democrat who tries to find practical approaches to solving problems in Finnish society.

Born in Helsinki "on the wrong side of the tracks," she grew up with a severe speech disability that taught her to be tolerant of differences in others. She has headed SETA, the main lesbian, gay, bisexual, and transgender rights organization in Finland, and is also a strong supporter of human rights and international unity. One Finnish teen said:

The thing I like the most about being a teenager in Finland is the amount of possibilities you can have here. *You can become almost anything you want to. I can't think of anything negative about living here.*

Finns at Work

The typical Finnish workday starts at 8 A.M. and ends at 4:30 P.M., Monday through Friday, though many can be seen at their desks until 5:30 or 6 P.M. Workers are given five or six weeks of paid vacation per year. In the majority of Finnish families, both parents have full-time jobs, no matter how many children they have. More than 70 percent of Finnish women of working age work full time. When Finnish couples decide to have children, they can rely on one of the best support

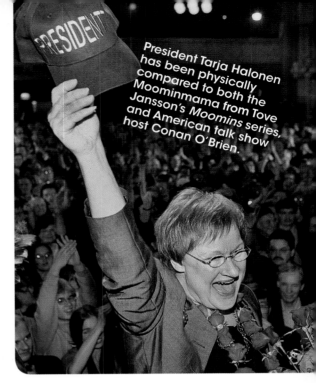

President Tarja Halonen has been physically compared to both the Moominmama from Tove Jansson's Moomins series, and American talk show host Conan O'Brien.

A Classless Society?

The differences between rich and poor families are less noticeable in Finland than in many countries. Part of the reason is the Finnish people's modesty. Even if they are very wealthy, they tend not to flaunt their good fortune. Also, those who have less money can rely on the government for many of their basic needs. There is assistance for food, clothing, and housing. Even the poorest Finns have a quality of life that makes it seem as though they have more income than they actually do.

systems in the world. Finnish parents get a generous amount of paid time off from work—an average of 11 months—when a new baby is born or adopted into the family.

Leading Industries and Occupations

Much of Finland is covered by forests, and much of the rest is farmland. For generations, that meant logging and farming were the leading industries and careers for young Finns. Finns who did not take up a career in farming could be expected to take on a trade related to the timber industry.

As logging and farming became more automated, fewer young people looked there for jobs . There was a shift toward modern technology, and Finns have been at the forefront of this industry. Finland was one of the first countries in the world to build a national wireless telephone network. And it

Short-Term Stay-at-Homes

During the past 40 years, the government has made life easier for new parents. With 105 days of maternity leave, six to 30 days of paternity leave, or 158 days of parental leave (which can be used by both the mother and the father), Finns are finding it easier to combine work and family life. The parent on leave receives, on average, an allowance of 66 percent of his or her previous income. Municipal day care is guaranteed for all children too young for school. If they cannot find a place in a municipal day care, parents are entitled to take child-care leave after the initial parental leave has ended. Recently parents have also been allowed to choose private day care centers, partly paid for by the government.

Parents of young children are also given the option of staying at home with the children until they turn 3. The parent is paid a home care allowance to make up for lost income. All the while, the parents' jobs are secure.

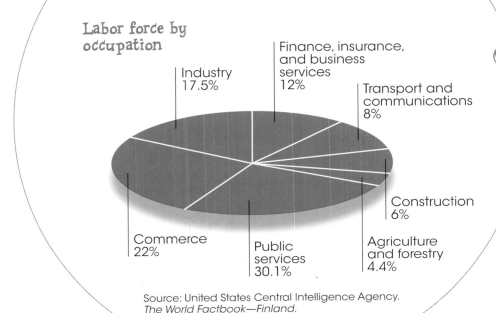

Labor force by occupation

- Industry 17.5%
- Finance, insurance, and business services 12%
- Transport and communications 8%
- Construction 6%
- Agriculture and forestry 4.4%
- Public services 30.1%
- Commerce 22%

Source: United States Central Intelligence Agency. *The World Factbook—Finland.*

was among the earliest to bring in broadband (high-speed) Internet service. An emphasis on new technology has exposed most young Finns to computers at an early age. That exposure has encouraged many of them to pursue careers in high-tech fields.

Nokia is one Finnish company that has taken advantage of the country's advances in technology. Nokia began as a paper and rubber maker in southwestern Finland in 1865. Since then, it has grown to be

Sharing its name with a small town in western Finland, Nokia has been named the best employer and brand in the country many times.

one of the world's leading telecommunications companies, with a popular line of cellular phones and 68,000 employees around the globe, including 24,000 employees in Finland. In 2005, the company sold its billionth phone. Other leading industries are energy, steel manufacturing, textiles, engineering, and design.

High-Tech Teens

Finns are among the heaviest cell phone users in the world, and teens are no exception. Kids talk on the phones with their parents and friends—almost any place and any time. They can use them to operate vending machines. By punching a few numbers into their phones next to a vending machine, the machines can dispense candy, a soda, or a bag of chips! The cost of the item will appear on the next cell phone bill. Those strapped for cash can even apply for bank loans at the touch of a button.

Text messages have opened new lines of communication. In 2007, a novel called *Last Messages* was written by a Finnish author. The 332-page book

As Finland's technology gets more advanced, new marketing channels are explored to bring tourists into the country.

is entirely in SMS text messaging format. And Finland's prime minister became a tabloid newspaper target after breaking up with a girlfriend through texting.

Finland is also home to a large number of Internet cafes and wi-fi hot-spots—wireless areas where teens can check their e-mail, instant-message each other, or cruise the Web.

The Finnish Handshake

The Finns are fond of long, warm greetings that usually include a firm handshake. It is customary to shake hands when meeting somebody new and to keep shaking hands as you share your names. Even family members and longtime friends, when meeting each other, will shake hands when they say hello and goodbye. In business situations, a good handshake is a sign of trust and honesty. Men tend to have very strong handshakes, while women use a weaker grip. Hugging and kisses on the cheeks are becoming more common as well.

Tourism and Travel

When Finns are not at work, they are probably not at home either. Finns love to travel with their families, and Finnish teens enjoy the time away from the rigors of school and homework. On weekends, they might spend time at their cabin or lake cottage. For longer vacations, Finns are inclined to take trips in Europe or overseas.

Some popular destinations for teens and their families are most parts of Europe, the beaches in Thailand, the Canary Islands, New York, and Florida. They visit historical sites or find warm beaches to get some sun in the midst of the long, dark Finnish winters.

Many Finnish teens participate in work or student exchanges, getting jobs or taking courses around the world.

Getting Around

Traffic in Finland is minimal in the countryside and smaller cities and remains manageable in larger cities, thanks to the widespread use of bicycles, buses, and trains. Since most families have only one car, and children find their own way to school, there is never really a rush hour, although some routes in and out of Helsinki are worse than others. Part of the reason cars are so rare is that gasoline is expensive. Average gas prices in Finland rose to 1.35 euros per liter (U.S.$7.30 per gallon) in 2007, compared with 0.62 euros per liter (U.S.$3.34 per gallon) in the United States. Finns have alternative ways to get

Caution: Reindeer Ahead

Reindeer and moose are common throughout Finland, which can make them a hazard to motorists. These animals rarely respond to car horns, acting as though they have just as much right to the roadway as a car.

Each year, reindeer and moose are responsible for more than 4,000 automotive accidents on Finland's roads and highways. Drivers are required to tell the police anytime there is an accident involving a reindeer or a moose. Watch out, especially if you are driving in November and December or July and August. Those are the two seasons when reindeer and moose tend to wander along the roadways.

around, and many would rather spend gas money on something else.

In winter, cars are required to have snow tires or all-weather tires. Some tires merely have extra traction, while others have small metal spikes sprouting from their treads. Those spikes come in handy on icy roads—or on roads made entirely of ice. When the ice on a lake is thick enough, Finns clear a path from

Reindeer and moose collision insurance is a must when driving in Finland.

one side to the other so they don't have to drive all the way around the lake. These ice roads are treated just like regular roads, some with speed limits and stop signs.

Finnish teens cannot get their driver's license until they are 18 years old. At 15, teens can apply for a license to drive a moped or a motorboat. Bicycles are the favorite way for teens to get around. They also rely on the extensive city bus systems, or they just walk.

For longer journeys, a vast network of trains helps Finns travel across the country or into neighboring countries at a reasonable cost. Trains are modern, roomy, quiet, and comfortable. Many cross-country trains have restaurants, bars, private suites, and sleeping compartments.

Biking to Work

Many Finns bicycle to work. Some get on their bikes year-round. Finland is relatively flat, making pedaling easy. Employers may provide their workers with changing rooms, saunas, showers, and lockers to make biking more appealing. Most Finnish cities have many dedicated bike paths and lanes. Helsinki alone has 496 miles (794 km) of two-way paths for bike riders, which is convenient but also dangerous. The number of injury-causing bicycle-related accidents per mile is five times as high as it is for car traffic and 10 times that of bus traffic.

Finns celebrate many sporting events, from football to hockey to the World Wife-Carrying Championships.

6

A Life of Leisure

WITH SUCH A STRONG EMPHASIS ON STUDIES, FINNISH TEENS SAVOR THEIR FREE TIME. Fortunately, there are a lot of ways they can spend it.

Klaus Castren, a 16-year-old boy in Kauniainen, said: After school has ended—and I don't have any particular reason to be at home doing any school work—it is quite possible that I can be found in the Road House restaurant eating a kebab or a pizza. Or equally possible is that I am hanging out in the local shopping mall Iso Omena (which means Big Apple in English).

Youth clubs are also popular—and free—places for teens to spend time playing games, practicing with a budding rock band, watching movies, or chatting over a cup of coffee. Most of the clubs are supervised by young adults who help coordinate many of the activities, tutor the teens, or help them with any problems they might have. Young Finns often call these clubs "work camps," especially when activities involve woodcutting, berry picking, cleaning, or washing rags.

Public swimming pools, indoor ice rinks, athletic fields,

and tracks are all either free or cost little to use. Sports clubs work hard to attract new players.

Because they love to learn, many teens take courses that are not required but simply interest them. They study foreign languages and cultures, or pick up a traditional Finnish handicraft, such as sewing, knitting, or carving.

On weekends, Finnish teens flock to their downtown areas to meet, chat, and flirt with each other. While they must be 18 to enter bars and pubs, there are many dance clubs open to minors. At the Youth and Cultural Centre of Oulu, there is a disco every Friday night for young people over 15. Another youth center is open from 2 P.M. until midnight from Tuesday to Sunday, and it provides a safe, drug-free place for teens to hang out, play games, and relax.

When the weather is right—and even when it is not—teens are glad to be outside. Cross-country skiing has once again gained popularity as a healthful exercise for teens. Skiiers use long, skinny skis and poles to glide across flat, snowy terrain, through forests, and across frozen lakes. It is a physically demanding sport, but one that has remained a Finnish tradition for centuries. However, snowboarding and downhill skiing are still the most popular snow sports among teens.

Snowmobiling also attracts Finns and their families. Finland has hundreds of miles of snowmobile trails in many parts of the country. For some, snowmo-

Finnish Youth Cooperation Alliansi

Friends have gathered in groups for as long as there have been groups to gather in. Few teens in the world meet as formally as Finnish teens who belong to Finnish Youth Cooperation Alliansi. Established in 1992, Alliansi merged three youth organizations under one umbrella. Today there are more than 100 member groups that belong to Alliansi. These groups provide educational programs, information networks, support for youth workers, and opportunities to travel abroad.

Finland is a popular tourist destination for winter sports enthusiasts.

biling is more than a form of recreation. When snow is heavy and roads are not plowed, snowmobiling is the only mode of transportation in extremely remote regions.

Sporting Silliness

Finns are fond of offbeat, silly, and strange sports. And what could be sillier and stranger than wife-carrying? Since 1992, the small town of Sonkajärvi in central Finland has hosted the World Wife-Carrying Championships. A husband hoists his wife—or any woman over the age of 16—on his back and carries her over a grueling course of sand, grass, asphalt, and deep water. The man with the fastest time wins.

Besides the Wife-Carrying Championships, there is also a team event, in which three men carry the wife in turns, and a 330-foot (100 m) wife-carrying sprint.

The winner gets to take home his wife's weight in beer, a bag full of "wife-carrying products," and a trophy.

First played in 1998, swamp soccer was said to have been invented by skiiers who wanted a sport to play in the summer. They took a ball to a swampy field and played soccer in the knee-deep mud. Today the biggest swamp soccer arena is in northern Finland, and more than 500 matches are held there during the Swamp Soccer World Championships every June.

After a muddy game of soccer, there's nothing like a hot sauna! The World Sauna Championships is Finland's hottest competition. Competitors are measured on how long they can stay in an extra hot, 230 F (110 C) sauna. For comparison, water boils at 212 F (100 C). The winner of the 2007 men's competition braved the heat for 12 minutes, 26 seconds, while the women's champion lasted 10 minutes, 31 seconds.

The World Mobile-Phone Throwing Championships set two records in 2005 when more than 3,000 spectators showed up to watch the winning throw of 313.4 feet (94.97 m). Contestants chuck a cell phone as far as they can. The winner receives a new cell phone.

How Many Lakes?

Thousands of years ago, when Finland was covered by huge glaciers, the

A LIFE OF LEISURE

temperature began to rise. As the glaciers slowly melted and retreated, the water gouged out big chunks of land. That unique process helped carve out Finland's seemingly countless lakes.

Situated next to those lakes—and rivers and streams—are more than 400,000 cabins and cottages. Finnish families adore leaving their regular homes and spending weekends and vacations at the cabin. There parents often spend time reading, while teens go swimming or waterskiing.

The lakes provide an endless source of recreation and entertainment—not to mention a place to cool off after spending time in a steamy sauna. In the summer, Finnish teens flock to lakes with beaches for long

There's no better way to cool off after a hot sauna than an ice swim! More than 120,000 Finns belong to ice swimming clubs.

The Aurora Borealis

The aurora borealis—also called the northern lights—is a fascinating light show that ripples across the night sky in Finland's northern regions. The colorful light is caused when particles from the sun collide with the atmosphere of Earth. Finns call the light displays "foxfire" because of an ancient belief that the mysterious lights came from a fox striking up fire with its tail or tossing snow into the sky.

Rods, Reels, and Rapalas

A lot of lakes means a lot of fish—and Finns love fishing. It is a popular pastime for families and children of all ages. If you open a tackle box, you are likely to find a Finnish-made Rapala fishing lure inside. Around the world, Rapala is a favorite lure among casual and serious anglers.

The Rapala lure was invented in the 1930s, when a fisherman noticed that big fish liked to eat smaller fish, especially wounded ones. Lauri Rapala went to his workshop and whittled, carved, and shaved a lure to look like a hurt minnow swimming in the water. His first lure was made of cork and covered with foil from chocolate bars. Legend has it he caught 6,000 pounds (2,700 kg) of fish on that first lure, and "the wiggle fish can't resist" was born.

Today customers in more than 140 countries buy 20 million Rapala lures a year, making Rapala the leading brand in fishing lures.

afternoons of swimming, sunbathing, and sailing on the cool, dark waters.

The lakes continue to attract teens and their families in the winter. Ice swimming is a fairly recent pastime for Finns of all ages. They find openings in icy lakes or frigid rivers and jump in! The icy dip is said to stimulate blood circulation and invigorate the body.

Finns also camp on frozen lakes in the winter to do some ice fishing, which is popular. No permit is required in Finland to fish with a hook and line, or for ice fishing—but it is needed to fish with a lure or net.

When they are not enjoying an outdoor activity, Finnish teens might make their way to a movie theater. Finland's movie industry is small, but movies are a popular pastime for teens, especially those on dates. More than 80 percent of films shown in Finland are made in other countries.

Relaxing at Home

A 14-year-old girl hurries home from school and settles down in a cushy chair. She unzips her knapsack and slides out a book by her favorite author, Mika Wickström, whose novels feature modern subjects. In Wickström's *Against the Grain*, a young girl is forced to choose between her eco-terrorist friends and her parents' fur business. It's a page-turner, and the girl reads until her mother interrupts her for dinner.

The same routine is repeated in homes throughout Finland, where every

Finns, like others around the world, fell in love with Harry Potter. When Harry Potter and the Order of the Phoenix was translated into Finnish in 2004, it sold 170,200 copies and became Finland's best-selling book of children's literature. In comparison, the second best-selling book was a collection of Finnish children's poems, which sold 60,000 copies.

latest book, they are likely to spend some time watching TV. Two national TV channels—TV1 and TV2—provide news, entertainment, and sports programs, which are shown in Finnish and Swedish. Two commercial channels—MTV3 and Nelonen—broadcast English-language shows from Great Britain and the United States. Satellite channels come in from all over the world.

Finns enjoy watching sports almost as much as playing them. They especially like watching football (soccer) matches and following Formula One racing. Finland's own Kimi Räikkönen was a runner-up in the 2005 Formula One World Driving Championships. Families often settle in to watch an afternoon of racing on TV.

The Winter Olympics rolls around every four years, and when it does, Finns tune in with a passion. They are likely to see many of their fellow Finns do well in cross-country and downhill skiing, speed skating, and hockey.

Every city and town has its own radio station. Four national radio stations broadcast in Finland. In Helsinki, Capital FM provides programs in English from BBC World News, Voice of America, and Radio Australia. For young people, X3M (Radio Extrem) is a favorite, featuring hard-rock music and live concert broadcasts. The NRJ station plays most of the Top 40 hits of the day.

Favorite rock bands usually feature standard rock beats and traditional Finnish melodies and lyrics. Most hit

teen can read. Literature for young Finns is increasingly reflecting their lives and modern society. There are also a growing number of fantasy novels for young readers, and Silja Kiehelä and Sari Peltoniemi are among the favorite authors of that kind of books.

When the winter weather gets too harsh, and teens have finished their

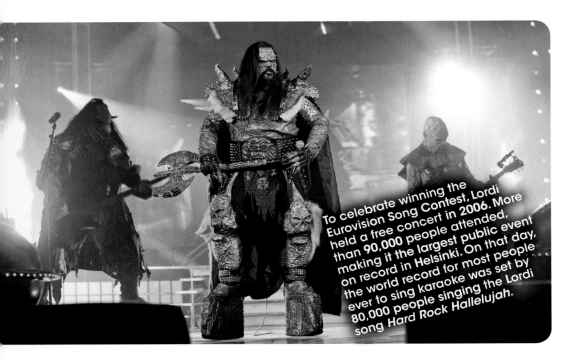

To celebrate winning the Eurovision Song Contest, Lordi held a free concert in 2006. More than 90,000 people attended, making it the largest public event on record in Helsinki. On that day, the world record for most people ever to sing karaoke was set by 80,000 people singing the Lordi song *Hard Rock Hallelujah*.

songs in Finland are sung in Finnish. For teens, top bands include HIM (a rock/metal band), Darude (a techno-dance band), and The Rasmus and The Crash (melodic pop). Heavy Finnish rock is also enjoying a resurgence with the likes of Children of Bodom, Nightwish, and The 69Eyes. Monster-rock band Lordi was given a special award from President Tarja Halonen for exemplary Finnish work in 2006.

The most famous composer in Finnish history was not quite as loud as Lordi. Jean Sibelius is still considered the king of Finnish classical music. He lived from 1865 to 1957 and composed dozens of songs and compositions for piano, violin, organs and symphony orchestras. At the height of his career, he was the world's favorite living composer.

Traditional Finnish music still holds a high place in Finnish culture. Some of the music, like Sami and Eastern folk songs, can include chanting or tonal singing. Fiddles, clarinets, accordions, and the *kantele*, a string instrument, are often used. Some families still play traditional instruments and sing Finnish folk songs together.

Saunas are Hot

Finns are famed for their saunas, or hot rooms, where one sits and sweats. As a Finnish saying goes, "First build the sauna. Then build the house." Nationally, there is an average of one sauna for every Finnish household.

Saunas can be a room inside the house or a separate building outside. They are usually made of aspen wood, which does not get too hot to touch or sit on. There is a small stove, called a *kiuas,* with rocks on top of it. Water is scooped from a bucket and dumped on the hot rocks to create steam. The temperature in a sauna is usually between a steamy 176 and 194 F (80 and 90 C).

Children continue the tradition by sitting in saunas with their families, starting at an early age. Most Finns enjoy their saunas naked, but some wear a towel or bathing suit. Sometimes in the sauna, they swat their backs, arms, and legs with small, leafy bundles of branches from a birch tree. The combination of sweat and birch-branch hitting is considered good for blood circulation and general health.

Finns also have sauna parties. Friends and neighbors are invited to sit in the sauna and take turns jumping into a nearby icy lake to cool off.

kantele
(khan-tele)
kiuas
(ki-uu-as)

There are many rules to uphold while in the sauna. One Finnish proverb says that people should behave in the sauna as they would behave in church.

Looking Ahead

TEENS IN FINLAND SHARE A LOVE OF LEARNING, READING, AND RECREATION. They could grab blankets and huddle indoors to escape the long, cold winters, but they do not. They embrace their environment, ready to take whatever the weather has to offer. They savor a good sauna, spicy sausage, and skiing. They take to the lakes whether it is sunny or snowing. They follow Finland's fashion and music trends, dress well to go out, and stay at the forefront of technology.

Teens enjoy time with their family, but their early independence prepares them for a life on their own. They are self-sufficient, strong, and straightforward, with a deep sense of national pride. They love to travel abroad and learn about other cultures, but they still respect their Finnish roots. These are the teens who live in Finland.

At a Glance

Official name: Republic of Finland

Capital: Helsinki

People

Population: 5,238,460

Population by age group:
0–14 years: 16.9%
15–64 years: 66.7%
65 years and over: 16.4%

Life expectancy at birth: 78.5 years

Official languages: Finnish and Swedish

Other common languages: English and Russian

Religions:
Lutheran Church of Finland: 84.2%
Orthodox: 1.1%
Other Christian: 1.1%
Other: 0.1%
None: 13.5%

Legal ages
Alcohol consumption: 18
Driver's license: 18
Employment: 14 with restricted hours; 16 without
Leave school: 16
Marriage: 18
Military service: 18
Voting: 18

Government

Type of government: Republic

Chief of state: President, elected by popular vote

Head of government: Prime minister, appointed by president

Lawmaking body: Unicameral Parliament, popularly elected

Administrative divisions: Six provinces

Independence: December 6, 1917 (from Russia)

National symbols: Flag is white with a blue cross extending to the edges. The colors of the flag symbolize the country's blue lakes and white snow, while the cross represents its affiliation with other Nordic countries whose flags also feature a cross.

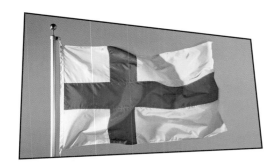

Geography

Total Area: 135,258 square miles (338,145 square kilometers)

Climate: Cold temperate; potentially subarctic but relatively mild because of the North Atlantic current, Baltic Sea, and more than 188,000 lakes

Highest point: Haltiatunturi, 4,357 feet (1,329 meters)

Lowest point: Baltic Sea, sea level

Major rivers and lakes: Kemijoki River, Lake Saimaa

Major landforms: Mostly low, flat to rolling plains interspersed with lakes and low hills

Economy

Currency: Euro

Population below poverty line: 12%

Major natural resources: Timber, iron ore, copper, lead, zinc, chromite, nickel, gold, silver, limestone

Major agricultural products: Barley, wheat, sugar beets, potatoes, dairy cattle, fish

Major exports: Machinery and equipment, chemicals, metals, timber, paper, pulp

Major imports: Foodstuffs, petroleum and petroleum products, chemicals, transportation equipment, iron and steel, machinery, textile yarn and fabrics, grains

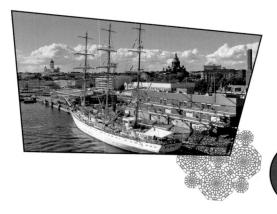

Historical Timeline

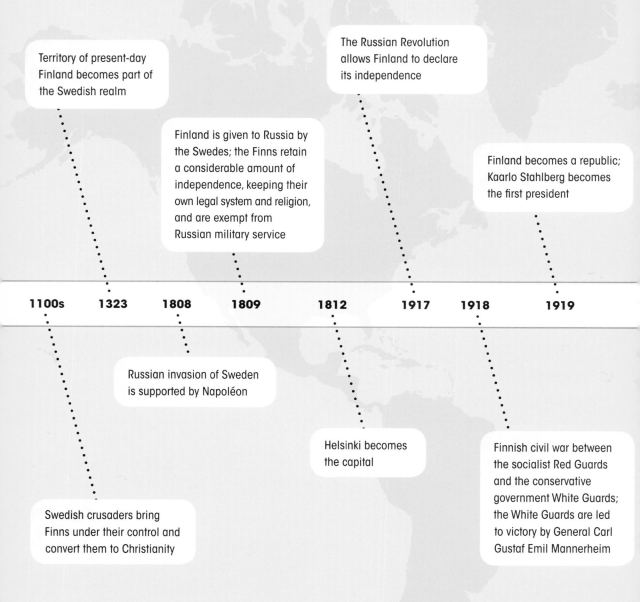

Territory of present-day Finland becomes part of the Swedish realm

The Russian Revolution allows Finland to declare its independence

Finland is given to Russia by the Swedes; the Finns retain a considerable amount of independence, keeping their own legal system and religion, and are exempt from Russian military service

Finland becomes a republic; Kaarlo Stahlberg becomes the first president

| 1100s | 1323 | 1808 | 1809 | 1812 | 1917 | 1918 | 1919 |

Russian invasion of Sweden is supported by Napoléon

Helsinki becomes the capital

Finnish civil war between the socialist Red Guards and the conservative government White Guards; the White Guards are led to victory by General Carl Gustaf Emil Mannerheim

Swedish crusaders bring Finns under their control and convert them to Christianity

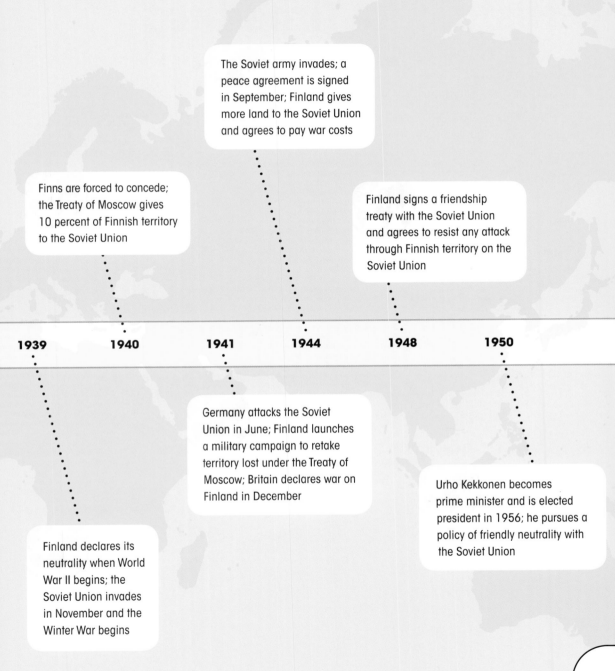

The Soviet army invades; a peace agreement is signed in September; Finland gives more land to the Soviet Union and agrees to pay war costs

Finns are forced to concede; the Treaty of Moscow gives 10 percent of Finnish territory to the Soviet Union

Finland signs a friendship treaty with the Soviet Union and agrees to resist any attack through Finnish territory on the Soviet Union

1939   **1940**   **1941**   **1944**   **1948**   **1950**

Germany attacks the Soviet Union in June; Finland launches a military campaign to retake territory lost under the Treaty of Moscow; Britain declares war on Finland in December

Urho Kekkonen becomes prime minister and is elected president in 1956; he pursues a policy of friendly neutrality with the Soviet Union

Finland declares its neutrality when World War II begins; the Soviet Union invades in November and the Winter War begins

Historical Timeline

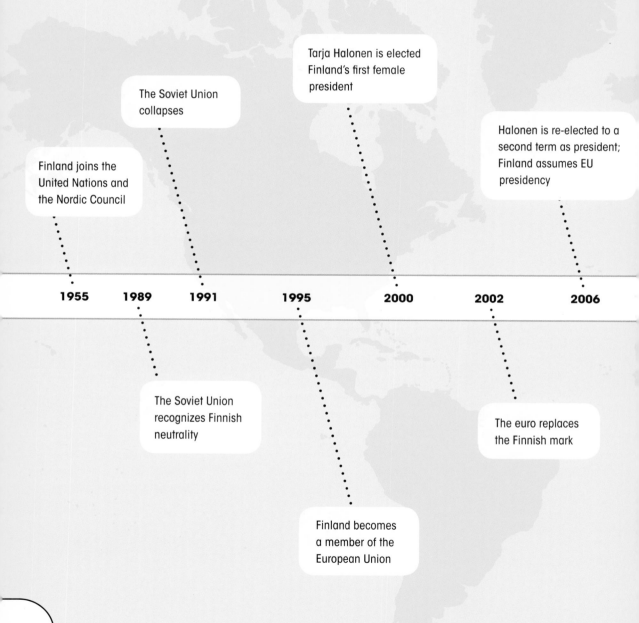

Tarja Halonen is elected Finland's first female president

The Soviet Union collapses

Halonen is re-elected to a second term as president; Finland assumes EU presidency

Finland joins the United Nations and the Nordic Council

1955   **1989**   **1991**   **1995**   **2000**   **2002**   **2006**

The Soviet Union recognizes Finnish neutrality

The euro replaces the Finnish mark

Finland becomes a member of the European Union

Glossary

comprehensive school | secondary education available to everyone

floor ball | indoor team sport similar to hockey; played with sticks and a ball

gross domestic product | the total value of all goods and services produced in a country during a period

missionaries | people who travel to spread a religion

Sami | original people of Finland and other northern European countries; formerly called Lapps

sauna | hot, steamy room used for relaxing

Scandinavia | region of northern Europe consisting of Norway, Sweden, Denmark, Finland, Iceland, and the Faeroe Islands

technical school | school concentrating on mechanical and industrial arts and applied sciences

temperate | mild weather, free from extreme heat or cold

Additional Resources

IN THE LIBRARY

Fiction and nonfiction titles to enhance your introduction to teens in Finland, past and present.

Durbin, William. *The Darkest Evening.* New York: Orchard Books, 2004.

Moomin: The Complete Tove Jansson Comic Strip. Montreal, Quebec: Drawn and Quarterly, 2006.

Schwartz, Carol. *The Maiden of Northland: A Hero Tale of Finland.* New York: Atheneum Books for Young Readers, 1996.

Brashares, Ann. *Linus Torvalds: Software Rebel.* Brookfield, Conn.: Twenty-First Century Books, 2001.

Leney, Terttu. *Finland: A Quick Guide to Customs & Etiquette.* Portland, Ore.: Graphic Arts Center Publishing, 2005.

Sia, Nicole. *Finland.* Philadelphia: Mason Crest Publishers, 2006.

ON THE WEB

For more information on this topic, use FactHound.

1. Go to www.facthound.com
2. Type in this book ID: 0756534054
3. Click on the Fetch It button.

Look for more Global Connections books.

Source Notes

Page 30, column 1, line 12: E-mail interview, Katariina Rauko. 1 March 2007.

Page 35, sidebar, column 2, line 3: "Refillable bottles are effectively recycled in Finland—Recycling Rate 98.7%." Sinebrychoff: Carlsberg Breweries. 24 June 2004. 10 July 2007. www.koff.fi/en/news/info/439.html

Page 43, column 1, line 10: E-mail interview, Kaisa Pakarinen. 5 March 2007.

Page 64, column 1, line 35: E-mail interview, Ville Luostarinen. 10 March 2007.

Page 73, column 1, line 9: E-mail interview, Klaus Castren. 2 March 2007.

Pages 84–85, At a Glance: United States Central Intelligence Agency. *The World Factbook—Finland*. 19 July 2007. 23 July 2007. www.cia.gov/library/publications/the-world-factbook/geos/fi.html

Select Bibliography

CIA World Factbook Online. *Finland*. 19 July 2007. 23 July 2007.
www.cia.gov/library/publications/the-world-factbook/geos/fi.html

Embassy of Finland. "Project Finland: A Student Guide for Action." *Project Finland*.
27 Sept. 2007. www.projectfinland.org/

Encyclopedia of Food and Culture. New York: Scribner/Thomson Gale, 2003.

Facts About Finland. Finland.com. 2004. 4 Sept. 2007. www.finland.com

Finland: History, Geography, Government, and Culture. Infoplease.com. 2007.
15 Sept. 2007. www.infoplease.com/ipa/A0107513.html

Finnish Language and Culture at the University of California, Berkeley. *Finnish
Studies*. 2005. 3 Oct. 2007. http://ies.berkeley.edu/fsp/finnishstudies/

Finnish Museum of Natural History. 24 Sept. 2007. 2 Oct. 2007. www.fmnh.
helsinki.fi/english/

Finnish National Board of Education. *The Education System of Finland*.
20 March 2007. 13 September 2007. www.oph.fi/english/SubPage.
asp?path=447,4699

Finnish Tourism Board. *Finland: The Official Travel and Tourism Guide*.
4 Sept. 2007. 10 Sept. 2007. www.visitfinland.com

Helsingin Sanomat: International Edition. 3 Oct. 2007.
www.hs.fi/english/

Klinge, Matti. *A Brief History of Finland*. Helsinki, Finland: Otava
Publishing Company Ltd., 1992.

Lankford, Mary D. *Birthdays Around the World*. New York: Harper
Collins, 2002.

Lavery, Jason Edward. *The History of Finland*. Westport, Conn.:
Greenwood Press, 2006.

Ministry of Finance and Foreign Affairs. *Finland*. 4 January
2004. 15 Sept. 2007. www.finland.fi

President of the Republic of Finland. "President of the Republic Tarja Halonen Answers Children's Questions." The President of Finland. 27 Sept. 2007. 28 Sept. 2007. www.presidentti.fi/netcomm/news/ShowArticle.asp?intNWSAID=43033&LAN=FI

Singleton, Fred. *A Short History of Finland.* New York: Cambridge University Press, 1995.

Statistics Finland. 21 June 2005. 15 June 2007. www.stat.fi/index_en.html

Suomi.fi. 22 Dec. 2006. 15 May 2007. www.suomi.fi/suomifi/english/index.html

Swallo, Deborah. *Culture Shock: Finland— A Guide to Customs and Etiquette.* Portland, Ore.: Graphic Arts Center Publishing, 2001.

Tuomainen, Sirpa. "Mustikka." 29 Sept. 2007. 1 Oct. 2007. http://mustikkasf.vuodatus.net/

Virtual Finland. 2007. 20 June 2007. http://virtual.finland.fi/

World Education Encyclopedia. Farmington Hills, Mich.: Thomson Gale, 2002.

Index

About the Author
Jason Skog

Jason Skog lives in Brooklyn, New York, with his wife and son. He has written several books for young readers. He was a newspaper reporter for 11 years and is now a freelance author and writer for magazines and newspapers, including *The New York Times*, the *Boston Globe,* and the *Baltimore Sun.*

About the Content Adviser
Sirpa Tuomainen

Sirpa Tuomainen is a native of Finland who makes her home in Berkeley, California, where she lives with her husband and their four bilingual, bicultural children. She is the coordinator of Finnish Studies at the University of California, Berkeley, where she also teaches Finnish language and culture. She is working on a book of fictional stories about immigrant women from Finland.

border to border • teen to teen • border to border • teen to teen • border to border